UNCOVERING
AMERICA'S PAST

BY STEPHANIE SIGUE

Editorial Offices: Glenview, Illinois • Parsippany, New Jersey • New York, New York

Sales Offices: Needham, Massachusetts • Duluth, Georgia • Glenview, Illinois
Coppell, Texas • Sacramento, California • Mesa, Arizona

When an **archaeologist** begins to study a group of people, he or she hopes to answer certain questions. When and where did these people live? What can we learn about how they lived? What kinds of things did they leave behind?

Scientists know that people lived in North America for many centuries before Europeans came. These American Indians, or Native Americans, lived in each region of the country, from the Atlantic coast to the Pacific coast and from the Great Lakes to the Gulf of Mexico. Each region's natural resources were important to how they lived. What we know about how American Indians lived long ago comes from the work of archaeologists as well as the knowledge passed on to American Indians today.

Archaeologists work at a dig in Wenatchee, Washington.

This model shows an Iroquois longhouse.

American Indians of the Eastern Woodlands

One of the major groups of the Eastern Woodlands were the Iroquois. The name *Iroquois* is used to describe the members of several American Indian groups. These groups include the Mohawk, the Seneca, the Onondaga, and the Oneida. Each was a group living in the forested regions of the Eastern Woodlands.

The Iroquois were farmers who usually built their villages on high ground. This way they could more easily protect themselves against attacks.

Within each village the Iroquois built longhouses. A **longhouse** had living spaces as well as places for storing things. Each was about 20 feet wide and from 75 to 120 feet long. The frame was made of wooden poles and covered with tree bark.

As many as twelve families could live in a single longhouse. Each family had its own living space with raised platforms for sleeping and storage. Walls separated them from other families. There were cooking fires at the center of the longhouse.

In what is the present-day Southeastern United States, American Indians lived in towns and villages that had three common features. One feature was a round meetinghouse with a domed room where the town leaders met. Another feature was a central town square, or stomp ground, for special ceremonies. The third feature was a large court where games were played. Family homes were usually built around the village border.

This picture shows a Creek log house and its inhabitants.

The Seminole *chickee* was built on a platform to avoid flooding.

The Creek, the Chickasaw, the Choctaw, and the Cherokee all lived in the Southeast. These groups built plain rectangular dwellings. Their houses were made of wood with roofs made of reed-like plants or straw.

Originally part of the Creek, the Seminole lived in Florida, where it was hot, humid, and swampy. Some Seminole lived in small houses with open sides called *chickees*. They were built on platforms to avoid flooding during heavy rains. People hung cotton fabric from the beams to keep out bugs and rain.

This is how a Mandan village looked in the 1800s.

American Indians of the Great Plains

The Great Plains of the western and central United States were home to many groups of American Indians. Some were sedentary, meaning that they stayed in one place and left only to go on buffalo hunts. For most of the year they were farmers. These groups included the Pawnee, the Omaha, and the Osage. They all lived in earth **lodges**.

These lodges were square with a floor built below ground level. The walls and roof were made from wooden poles, which were covered with woven grass and mud. Beginning at the base, the builders applied a coat of mud. The mud kept the house warm in the winter and cool in the summer. An opening, or smoke hole, was left in the roof's center.

The Mandan and the Hidatsa lived in villages along the upper Missouri River in North Dakota. They built earth lodges. Some lodges were built near the river and others were built near the forests. These lodges were used when trees were used to make fires.

Each lodge had a dome shape. They were between forty and sixty feet wide and about fifteen feet high. Lodges had a roof made of wooden beams covered with willows, grass, and sod. There was a central fireplace inside where many social activities took place. Animal hides were used to separate the sleeping quarters from the rest of the house. A family kept all of its belongings inside the home, including dogs and horses. Horses were kept inside so they would not be stolen.

Changing Ways of Life

In the 1500s Spanish explorers brought horses with them to North America. Their arrival changed the ways of life of American Indians of the Great Plains. Horses made hunting easier and allowed American Indian groups to travel farther and faster. Over time, many of these groups became nomads who moved from place to place.

Most American Indian groups of the Great Plains were not sedentary. They were nomadic people who were always traveling. They hunted buffalo and followed the herds that moved across the region. The Sioux, the Cheyenne, the Comanche, the Blackfoot, and the Crow were some of the many nomadic groups who lived in the Great Plains.

The nomadic groups of the Great Plains created a home called the **tepee** that could be taken down easily, carried away, and rebuilt. It had a cone-shaped frame made from long, tall wooden poles that were tied together at the top and covered with buffalo hides. The hides, from buffalo that had shed their winter coats, were replaced once a year.

The first tepees were small. Trained dogs could help carry the poles and hides when a group moved. After the groups of the Great Plains began to use horses, however, their tepees became larger. With horses they could move their belongings more easily.

Moving Tepees

Tepees started off small, and trained dogs would carry the poles and hides when the group moved. After Spanish explorers brought horses to North America, the tepees became larger. With horses, American Indian groups of the Great Plains could move their tepees and belongings more easily.

Wickiups

Other nomadic groups built disposable homes. When they moved, they left these homes behind. The Paiute, the Shoshone, and the Ute groups lived on the Great Plateau between the Sierra Nevada and Rocky Mountains. They built wickiups, homes with a cone shape. They were made with a lightweight frame covered by grass.

Tepees were covered with buffalo hides. Once a year each tepee was covered with a new, fresh hide.

American Indians of the Desert Southwest

American Indians of the Desert Southwest built a variety of homes. The Mogollon (moh-GOH-yohn) and the Hohokam (huh-HO-kum) built pit houses that were partly under the ground. Each house was a rectangle with wooden poles that leaned inward to support a roof. This created walls that sloped. People covered the roof and walls with branches and grass and then with a layer of adobe, or mud.

American Indian cliff dwellings and **pueblos** are two of the most amazing finds made by archaeologists in the Desert Southwest. Cliff dwellings were found in an area called Mesa Verde (MAY-seh VEHR-dee). This is located in the "Four Corners" region of the United States where the present-day borders of Utah, Colorado, New

Mesa Verde's largest cliff dwelling is called the Cliff Palace, which has 217 rooms and 23 kivas. A *kiva* is a circular underground room used for religious ceremonies.

Mexico, and Arizona meet. An ancient group known as the Anasazi built these dramatic buildings, located below a **mesa** and set among steep cliffs. Some cliff dwellings are small and housed only a few families. Others are large apartment-like buildings where hundreds of people lived.

After the Anasazi left the Four Corners region, new communities formed farther south. The people who moved there built pueblos. A pueblo contains rooms that are stacked one on top of another. Each higher story is set back from the one below. People used ladders to move from one dwelling to another.

Large pueblos are called great houses. Some have hundreds of rooms. Some of the largest and most famous examples are in Chaco Canyon in New Mexico.

Art and Artifacts

Archaeologists are interested in more than just dwellings. They also look for **artifacts**, such as tools, weapons, clothing, pottery, and baskets—anything that can help them learn more about a culture.

Tools and weapons can tell scientists how people hunted for food. From the size and weight of a weapon, experts can tell how hunters used it.

People have found American Indian arrowheads all over the United States.

An eagle appears on the beadwork of a Tlingit (TLING-git) ceremonial robe in Alaska.

American Indians were—and are—expert weavers, potters, basket makers, and carvers. Scientists can date some of the American Indian artifacts found by archaeologists to prehistoric times.

Before Europeans arrived in the Northeast, American Indian women of the Eastern Woodlands made clothing from animal skins and decorated the clothing with porcupine quills. They often dyed the quills before sewing them onto a garment. When Europeans moved west they brought new materials with them, including glass beads. American Indian women began to use fancy beadwork to decorate their clothing.

The American Indians of the Pacific Northwest carved wooden **totem poles** to tell the story of a family tree. For example, a family might claim a relationship with a particular animal. That animal would be carved on the family's totem pole. Some totem poles are more than forty feet high.

This is an example of a totem pole found in the Pacific Northwest.

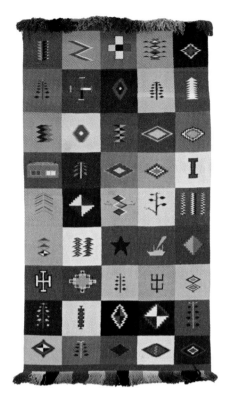

This Navajo blanket was made in the late 1800s.

In the Desert Southwest, some of the most famous Navajo weavings are chiefs' blankets. These works of art use patterns, such as stripes, zigzags, and diamond shapes.

Today many of the special objects made by American Indians are collected by people and museums around the world. The National Museum of the American Indian in Washington, D.C., contains more than 800,000 works. The pieces are from North and South America, and they cover a period of ten thousand years.

These artifacts, along with the histories passed on to American Indians today, contribute to our understanding of how American Indians of long ago lived.

Glossary

archaeologist a scientist who studies the artifacts of people who lived long ago and draws conclusions from them

artifact an object made by people in the past

lodge a large, round hut built by American Indian groups of the Great Plains

longhouse a building used for shelter by the Iroquois

mesa a high, flat landform that rises steeply from the land around it

pueblo an American Indian village of the Desert Southwest region of the United States, typically made up of stone or adobe dwellings

tepee a dwelling built by American Indians of the Great Plains

totem pole a wooden post carved with animals or other images; often made by American Indians of the Pacific Northwest to honor ancestors or special events